POETRY now

# *Symmetry In Verse*

Edited by

Heather Killingray

First published in Great Britain in 2004 by
*POETRY NOW*
Remus House,
Coltsfoot Drive,
Peterborough, PE2 9JX
Telephone (01733) 898101
Fax (01733) 313524



SB ISBN 1 84460 827 1

# *FOREWORD*

Although we are a nation of poets we are accused of not reading poetry, or buying poetry books. After many years of listening to the incessant gripes of poetry publishers, I can only assume that the books they publish, in general, are books that most people do not want to read.

Poetry should not be obscure, introverted, and as cryptic as a crossword puzzle: it is the poet's duty to reach out and embrace the world.

The world owes the poet nothing and we should not be expected to dig and delve into a rambling discourse searching for some inner meaning.

The reason we write poetry (and almost all of us do) is because we want to communicate: an ideal; an idea; or a specific feeling. Poetry is as essential in communication, as a letter; a radio; a telephone, and the main criterion for selecting the poems in this anthology is very simple: they communicate.

# *Contents*

## A Mother's Farewell

My Sons, O my Sons what is this that you see?
Is it the face of once a young mother so proud,
Or is it the face of just an old woman,
Lying here in a shroud?

My Sons, O my Sons I too was like you,
As I prayed by my mother and saw her life through.
Then my face was not wrinkled, my eyes saw the light,
My feet was so sprightly, and my arms held you tight.

My Sons, O my Sons I have missed you before!
When you left your own home for those far away shores,
Those days were so long, and the nights longer still,
As I prayed, and I watched those far away hills.

My Sons, O my Sons I too left my home -
To be close to my Sons, and not die alone
But I hoped and I prayed that one day we'd return,
To the home that we left, never more for to roam.

My Sons, O my Sons now I dream quite a lot
Of the home that we left, and friends I never forgot,
As I wander around all the old places I knew -
With the Sons that I love, and old friends too.

My Sons, O my Sons now do not despair,
For God in his mercy said, 'There is room for me there,'
And there I will pray for the ones I love dear,
Sure God he has told me, there is a place for you here.

My Sons, O my Sons I have a final request,
Please take me back home and there lay me to rest,
And there I will rest and contented I'll be
As I wait for my Sons where all will be free.

***Hugh Dempsey***

## From Where To Where

I've not got a compass, nor a map to read,
Nothing to tell me where each path leads,
And with each step I take, the deeper I go,
But to where? Or where from? I truly don't know.
This life is a maze full of crossroads and doors,
Wrong turns and dead ends, I stop. No more.
No footprints behind me, ever this point I return,
Around in a circle, what this time did I learn?
On my left, a door opens, whispers call from inside,
I look at your face, blank. All emotion you hide.
So now then, with this transient step that I take,
If I enter this portal, will you follow in my wake?
Silence. I'm deafened, you're a statue of stone,
I fear. You let me go. I step through, I'm alone.
Slowly the door closes, behind me, disappears,
Before me, a new crossroad. I've been here, my fears.

***Andrew Llewellyn***

# On The Page

Quickly photographing fleeting thoughts
Captured then as phrases to be wrought
Rescued from the blizzard of the head
Before they fade and melt and join the dead
Juggled shaped and frozen inky fresh
Developed on a page and laid to rest.

A concept slips so quickly through the mind
Nature's slippery inklings must we find
That carry tiny prints of nature's plans
To catalogue develop bind and brand
Laid carefully and edged with loving care
God's truth preserved indelibly to share.

Of other dreams the remnants lay in waste
The lights go out as we all leave this place
The tiny screams of truth that lay within
The ones we missed or threw into the bin
The cleaners shred and sack them all to burn
And never to this place will we return.

***Brin Parsons***

## THE COUNTRYSIDE

Low branches sweep the floor
blossom starting to appear on small young trees
swaying to the breeze or your voice
hills risen from even ground helping me to find you
so once again I could see your face
old hedgerows planted to help me find the way to your heart
but I'm just getting lost in my own head
the trails were left by me, looking for you day after day after day
the different colours of the tilted hills represent the moods day
in and out
green - looking good for finding you
brown - I know I've lost you forever
then fading into the low clouds
where the one true colour that made me realise who and where I was
old bushes cover the derelict buildings
in which I first saw your face.

***Steven Shortland***

## THE ROMANY CARAVAN

I love to travel the country road
With my shiny caravan,
With my horse Flossie in the reins
And my faithful dog called Dan.
Inside the van I humbly share
My wooden table and easy chair,
A cosy bed beside the fireside wall
And my tiny bookcase and wardrobe tall.
A tin kettle and a bucket clean
Where I can get water from a nearby stream,
Pots and pans and dishes galore,
And cups and saucers for my store.
Fleecy rugs strewn on the floor
And curtains fitted round the swinging door.
Farmers' yarns I love to hear
When I visit the local country fair.
As I go merrily on my way
I thank the Lord for each new day.

***Laura Chaplin***

## THE PANDA

The panda is a cute big bear
From them I have nothing to fear.
Oh, I know how you do
Love, to eat bamboo,
We have lots of bamboo here too.
They may be all for you.
I do not want you to be at the brink
Of being extinct.

***Immanuel Smith***

## THE SHELL

Today I stand a fragment of myself
High upon the study room shelf
I used to ride upon the high sea
Now I lay me upon this dead tree
My companions are these books
And various creatures caught in my nooks.

A spider had made me its home
No longer am I allowed to roam
I stand here a shell of myself
I sit here upon the study room shelf.

***Kareen Smith***

## The Troubles Are Not Over

It's such a shame there's violence here,
Derry has to live in so much constant fear!

I've had enough of stones being thrown at school buses
And sometimes children can't even get to school.

I can barely remember peace because those fools damaged it.

Derry still has so much violence on our streets,
Sometimes it can bring us close to defeat.
Many Derry children drink on the streets at night,
They shout and they fight.

Is alcohol the reason we lost it all?

Local people are attacked and that's a sad fact.
There's a lack of respect across Ireland,
But many of us just want to live a normal life.
Why must we suffer 'cause of sectarian thugs?

I cannot ignore the truth I see.
We want peace *but* the troubles are not over!

The soldiers that opened fire on Bloody Sunday still are not punished
And there's still shameful violence in the town.
Decent people are made to feel down.

The Bloody Sunday inquiry is costing millions!
But the truth isn't clear and people are still killing!
The relatives still insist the crowds were largely peaceful
And soldiers killed without justification.

Without a moment's hesitation I believe we could have peace.
Now many Derry children have so little.
Their education has so little.

The Omagh bombing created another nightmare.
It's not fair that our children pay the price,
But who cares about their quality of life?

The soldiers claim they didn't shoot until they were fired upon.
Now the dead are gone the battle still goes on . . .

The troubles are still going on and on . . .
More bombs are exploding and bullets killing.

Bill Clinton worked for peace here,
But we still have something to fear!

Sometimes it's easier to give up.
Oh *damn,* are we out of luck?
Our prayers were not yet answered but prayer takes time
And maybe one day we'll feel fine.

I just need God to somehow give us a sign that maybe one day
We'll have normal lives.

When children can't get to school 'cause of sectarian thugs
You see the disgrace we have to face.

I cannot understand why murderers kill on the grounds
Of someone's religion,
They don't deserve a moment's peace when they left
Their victim deceased.

A child is too often killed in sectarian violence.
It leaves a silence in the family's home and the child's school.
The fools that do it aren't doing what God wants.
Bloody Sunday will always haunt the streets of Derry.

Are we returning to Northern Ireland's darkest days?
News of the troubles reaches land so far away.
When I see children play I just have to say we could change our ways.

I don’t want to live among these dangerous thugs anymore.
The *Bloody Sunday* film made old wounds so sore.
It’s terrible that bombs are exploding and the world’s
Media reports the shame.
We need to know the truth of who’s responsible and who’s to blame.
I cannot ignore the truth I see.
The troubles are not over . . .

***Paul Curran***

## Show Them The Way Home

Let me put you in solitary confinement
Deprived of all your rights
Deprived of all your dignity
That will demonise your sanity.

Let me take you on a journey
The airs' aroma is melancholy
Stars dimly light a stony path
Luring minds and bodies forlorn
Flanked by hollow hearts
Into a dark corridor bereft of hope
That leads to brutality and terror.

Let me ask you how one human being
Can destroy another?
There are no answers
The question will remain.

Let me give you a ray of hope
For as an umbrella may perish and leak
Let in the rain
Perchance a rainbow may shine through
That could signpost their way home.

***Elaine Priscilla Kilshaw***

## CHATTERTON

Deceit and shame ended his game:
This poor sad youth abused the truth.

The gory sunrise
Spells his end
Paints his couch
In crimson blend.
The poisoned drops
Have stopped his heart:
At just sixteen
His life was art.

In his day
Such a death
Was not merely
End of breath.
No Holy ground
Allowed him in:
Self murder, then
Was mortal sin.

How ironic now, it seems,
This bitter end to youthful dreams,
That his dying grief and shame
Through art, should give him long-lived
*Fame.*

***Margaret Clary***

## The Journey

Lying here waiting with trepidation
The time is drawing near
It's the day of my operation
I admit, I am filled with fear.

The nurse she came to prepare me
For the operating table
It's to replace this blessed knee
Then hopefully I'll be able.

The time is here now, but don't worry
The trolley has arrived at last
So hop aboard, but there's no hurry
Even so it moves off fast.

The theatre looks large and daunting
Equipment sterile and clean
Along comes a man with a needle
That's the last thing I recall having seen.

Some time very much later, in recovery
I lie feeling strange, weird and unreal
I can hear the clock ticking
I have survived this tremendous ordeal.

To walk again like a normal person
Not to hobble and be in pain
It's been a very long journey
Now I have everything in life to gain.

*Gill D'Arcy*

## Out In The Garden

We look pretty in the garden,
In the sun,
We play different games all the time,
Out in the garden,
We play together all day,
Out in the garden,
We skip and run all day long,
Out in the garden,
We always find sometime to play,
Out in the garden,
We are always happy,
Out in the garden,
We are never alone or scared,
Out in the garden,
We are always happy,
Out in the garden.

***Heather Thompson (8)***

## You Go Alone

You go alone among the rocks
Breathing the destiny in the dawn
And scuttled red sky will inhale
Lapsed airs for the azure morning.

And when the spell gets broken
Through calm contemplation
I will close my eyes to heap
Some other vagrant image
And cliff tops will shout
Pointing to the vagaries
Of approaching shadows
Cast out by stiff necked sun.

Mouth upon mouth now tasting
Past memories without regret
Tongue upon tongue to explore
Clocked dark stone circled in fell.

For the movements of hills
Feeding cool waters to rivulets
Some stubborn songs even hiding
In order to burn like dry tinders.

***Durlabh Singh***

## On Show: Body Living, Spirit Dying

I am young and small but carefree,
Out enjoying the wilderness day.
We are fishing the river this morning,
To help hold our hunger at bay.
Though my catch is low, this is fun,
As the fish are good at escaping.
My parents do best at this game,
So I go on playing and chasing.

Then she awakes . . . it's only a dream,
The cruel, remembering sort.
Her mind begins the surrender,
Freedom lost, all her battles, have been fought.

Look at her, go on . . . stare that stare
But this time . . . look into her eyes.
See the depth of a lost child's despair,
Witness spirit, inch by inch, as it dies.
She is captured again . . . by your camera,
On film, does it show all the pain?
Let compassion shout and not whisper,
That her loss, can never be, a proud gain.
We are quick to say she is safe
But we keep her from life's thrilling dare
And as she madly rocks from side to side,
We forget . . . she was born . . . a wild bear.

***Madeleine Wilson***

## SUNDAY

When I was young on the Sabbath Day
We went to church, meeting friends on the way
We would chat, catch up on all of the news
Before taking our seats in one of the pews

Now on a Sunday to the boot sales they go
Tables lined up row upon row
Clothes, jewellery, plants, the odd book
Picking things up to have a close look

The money is spent, the bargains bought
It's up the road we all then trot
We gather round to have our tea
And settle down to watch TV

We did not go to church today
But still at night found time to pray
To thank God who from up above
Watched over us with tender love.

***Sheila Christie***

## WHERE LEAD LIES?

Came they touting at my door
Seeking to help my lot?
Like chameleon's changing mien
Later to deaf ears did I implore,
Listening only they to party plot,
Forgetting me - old has-been!

Ignoring all pleas, in mood perverse
PM backs Bush's rash and illegal war,
With groundless WMDs, now of course,
Heedless to his country's angry roar
'Gainst Middle Eastern curse
Of never-ending, bloody war.

Wily PM as with sly-eyed fox
Can any bird coax off any bough
When weasel words so softly flow
In legerdemain's neat double-cross
Of nation's trust by ways unorthodox,
Never answering what we need to know!

Will their hubris never recognise
The power of the people great
From whose roots their tenures rise
Answerable to the majesty of state
On which lies our democratic fate -
Not in subterfuge, nor devious lies!

***Ron Deen***

## HEADACHE PICTURE

Am I dreaming or am I really dead?
Am I married or am I even wed?
Has someone visited me in my bed?
Did I open that window with head full of lead?

Is it the morning with the sun shining in?
Is it the night when lights are all dim?
I'll feel so relaxed and so very tired,
Did I fling myself on the bed to be admired?

Am I waiting for my prince to ride by,
To carry me off into the sunset sky?
All this is too good to be ever true,
Sometimes happens to me and you.

Will I awake and see birds and trees?
Will I ever open my eyes and feel the breeze?
I wonder if I will awake at all
To get ready and go to the ball?

***Eileen Witt-Way***

## A Very Brief Encounter

I saw you on the cross-country train
When I was travelling south
And when you smiled and said, 'Hello,'
My heart was in my mouth.

You were so good looking
With fair hair and a gorgeous smile
And I was experiencing feelings
Which had lain dormant for many a while.

I find it very difficult
To describe what I was feeling
I only know that one look from you
Could send my senses reeling.

All too soon I reached my journey's end
And we had to say goodbye
I wonder what the outcome would have been
If I had said I had something in my eye.

Who knows, perhaps our paths will cross
When I travel south again
Until then I will have my memory
Of a very brief encounter on a train.

***Jackie Richardson***

## Unrequited Obsession

Can't get enough but that's what I crave
I'll search for the answer 'til I'm in my grave
You're the only one who can satisfy my need
I'll scratch at your surface 'til my fingers bleed
My body requires a daily dose to sedate
Which sends me into a comatose state
You're blissfully blind to my forever call
But you'll hear one day - you can't ignore them all
I always hold back from telling you
Because I'm told it's the right thing to do
But I promise you this, you will be mine
Even if I have to cross that line
So wait for the day when it all comes to the fore
The secret will out and you'll be mine forever more

You'll be mine forever more.

***Karen Cameron***

## OUR JOURNEY

We have faced a long journey together, both you and I.
We have fought the demons that continuously taunted our lives,
pushed us apart, doubted our faith and challenged our hearts.
And although we have not conquered them all,
we have somehow, managed to survive.

Together we created another chapter within this story,
within this journey called life.
Finally, a chance to change the past,
and start living the future, start living the rest of our lives.
We both accepted fate and marched on knowing what
could possibly come.

As we marched down that long, winding road together,
It might have appeared that I was brave,
It might have appeared that I knew how to be strong,
how to hold my head up, I knew where I belonged.
But in the core of my heart, where so few see,
I was so afraid, I was in agony.

Because there are things I wish I could've said,
And things I wish I hadn't.
There were times when I felt I almost knew you,
And times I know I didn't.
I will always wish for things to have been different,
And yet I will always be grateful they weren't.

***Danielle Watts***

## Million Miles (Final Act)

Shall I fall from rock unto river
Cry on your shoulder, defeated and bitter
Always pursuing a path so twisted
Crawl on gold, disguised with litter
Holdin' out for touch of a mother
Going under, my head asunder.

All I asked for was love for another
Fists are thumpin', but my heart's still pumpin'
Is this your fear, cos it's men I'm humpin'?
No more secrets for you to pursue
No more of the pain that I put you through
You may have been close
But I was always a million miles from you.

With all those words, feedin' the hurricane
With all those hurts, feedin' the pain
What more could I give you?
I hope you'll come soon
I swear I'll be waitin'
Now I'm a million miles from you.

***Graham Robson***

## CLOCKWORK BRAIN FODDER

When cracking open the chest the surgeon found no blood.
No organs pumping, no veins,
Only clockwork ticking and turning
And stringy stuff holding her in.

When he broke down the bricks in her brain,
He found only matter.
Grey, purple and snake-like,
Feelings and visions extinct,
And sieves draining abscessed emotion.

I am not her.
She's walking and sleeping and eating.
Inside - out of existence.
The surgeon's screws are twisting rustily,
Slipping out of their casing, sucking her in.
Unlocked. Unhinged. Unreal.

***Judith Horne***

## Perpetually Moored

Of the times in which I'm happy girl, you and only you can tell
and all the times in which I'm lonely only you can break the spell
you stay put in your quest to find truer meaning
yet the only way out is through leaving
clandestine workings of the way in which we live
and in staying put in the quest only you can fight back and learn to give
in all my life the wheels that turned have never been smooth
turning still, one day, I hope they improve
and deeper still in times of trouble
rise through the clouds and through the rubble
take the time to make the change,
it's up to you alone, find your way through the herds of the strange
back to the start, home feels like a shell
a forgotten place which once harboured an angel.

***Stuart Dolan***

## HOLIDAY 3000 - WISH YOU WERE HERE?

The holiday of the future,
Where would you go?
Mars?
The moon?
Or a recently discovered planet in a
Far corner of the galaxy?
What about Earth?
A choice between
A smog filled city,
Or a resort beneath a hole
In the ozone layer?
A country gasping for a drop of clean water,
Or one half destroyed by floods
Caused by melting ice caps?
A beach with no animals or
Birds to watch you sunbathe,
Or a country cottage on a desolate plain?
A rainforest turned to desert
By thoughtless humans,
Or a world controlled by politicians,
Driven by power, corrupted by greed?
Wish you were here?
I don't
But H is for holiday,
And H is for hope.

***Lucy Hancock (12)***

## Turkey Day

'Get your coat on love, it's turkey day today
Christmas is only a short week away
Off to market we go, I'll let you choose
We want the plumpest, no time to lose!'
'Mummy . . . was that once alive?'
'Yes dear.'
'Mummy . . . is it dead?'
'Yes dear!'
'Mummy . . . did it cry when it died?'
'No dear!'
'Mummy . . . how do you *know* what it said?
Did it *want* to die?
Did it scream and cry?
Are they all its sisters and brothers?
Are they girls or boys?
Did they make a noise?
Did they all have fathers and mothers?
Does it hurt to die?
Did they all say goodbye?
Is it just like going to sleep?
But you said killing is bad.
Mummy . . . I'm really sad.
I pray the Lord their souls to keep.
I don't want to eat turkey Mummy.'

***Bernie Jones***

## Follow My Heart

Here at the crossroads of life we must part
I have come this far with you
Now I must go on alone
Just to follow my heart.

Now as we say goodbye
You should know our love will never die
Under a star filled sky
We're not so far apart
As I'll always keep a place for you
So close to my heart.

Now it's written there somewhere
In those lines of fate
That I must be going now
That the hour is getting late.

And someone else waits at their window for me
Someone who I've been longing to see
So here at the crossroads of life we must part
I have come this far with you
Now I must go on alone
Just to follow my heart.

***K Lake***

## The Last Farewell

Walking through the park one night
I saw a sudden flash of light
Treading softly over twigs and grass
It was then I saw a blonde haired lass
As I approached and got very near
My body shook, so full of fear
Suddenly it was as black as pitch
And the blonde haired lass she was a witch
Chanting names and casting spells
Dancing around with rings and bells
Trying to raise her friends, the spooks
It was then I saw her evil looks
Shouting and screaming about their fates
Pleading for them to return as mates
Chanting about the frogs and bats
Within a circle of witches' hats
The ground then shook and to my alarm
Through the soil there came a hairy arm
It dragged her down without a trace
Screaming through her evil face
The good thing is she met her friends
Let's hope that this is where it ends.

***Paul Sullivan***

## DESPAIR

My stomach feels like a bottomless pit, filling with despair
For when I turn to speak to you, you are no longer there.

I want to cry but no tears will come
This lump in my throat it grows
You've left this, what we call life,
Gone to . . . well know one knows.

I hope there is a heaven
Which will gain from our sad loss,
Be at peace, be free, be happy with those before you
Whose path you did cross.

***Tracey Maria Milner***

## ALONE

I'm alone in my bed at night
I awake and give myself a fright
The shadows on the wall
So tall
Mean nothing
Yet something
I'm alone
In my home with no one
To care or share the sorrow
I feel in the dark of somebody missing
Is there anyone listening
To my cries?
The sadness in my eyes
Make me sleep, to weep
For the morning
A new day is dawning
So I awake to my heartache
To a new day
It's not all bad, it's not so sad
A new day for them it seems
But!
I'll still see the shadows in my dreams.

***G C Dymock***

## A Throw Of The Dice

Dead to the world, the life that teemed outside
The confines of the attic's gloom
Meant nothing now to him
Sprawled on the bed.
A trunk
That once had held good fortune stood beside
Him as light - striving to consume
The sorrow packed within -
Pushed in and shed
And sunk
Its rays into the gloom but lost and died
Beneath the sorrow and the room
Hid him. With one loose limb
He lay as dead.
Dead drunk.

***Diane Elizabeth Maltby***

## POWERFUL MINDS OVER CLENCHED FISTS

Although up above the sun will shine,
And like diamonds dazzle, the stars softly glisten,
A problem will always arise
Where no one alive will want to listen.

Problems occur all around the earth,
Even greatest men alive have nothing they can do,
Like a young child who's giving birth.
That young lady. A miniature of me and you.

We can't stop it, or fight it,
People fall like a shattered plate to pieces.
Why stop it, when in fact, we're the ones in life who provide it?
So those bloodstains on the wall, leave their dying traces.

I understand the obstacles in life, but focus, to this you need to listen,
To understand that the words cut much deeper than those shattered pieces on your wrist,
But remember, they are not but words, know that life works in the mind,
Not empty words to take over the clench of your fist.

Understand that the hand is fragile, bones quickly crack,
You see it cry, watch it drip, sweet child, feel it burn,
One moment of aggression, turns to a lifetime you will lack,
And with no one to notice, without you, forever will turn.

So listen to me, take pride in words that only I say,
Understand you can't fight it, but the mind can stop the dripping blood among your wrist,
Problems may arise, words come and go, and not fade away,
Just remember, the mind is stronger than the clench of your fist.

***Natasha Bayes***

## Up At The Old Church

High kings exchanged gold there
Burned into the soil that's history's rage
Except no chariots of fire found?
Before my time or yours I think,
Only a microcosm of wider civilisations
Crusades, wars, land grabbing
To the new age of fancy dress
And the hopeless espy of the week
That's for some other days dreaming
Or from the heart of scorched earth.

***M Trainor***

## UGG

He sits on his haunches
His face held in the palm of his hands
His sparse black hair points ever skywards!
No garment covers his modesty
A discerning smile hides his sorrow

***Pat Seddon***

## KEEP ON SMILING

Smiling is infectious
You can catch it like the flu
When someone smiled at me today
I started smiling too

I passed around the corner
And someone saw my grin
When he smiled I realised
I'd passed it on to him

I thought about that smile
And realised its worth
A single smile, just like mine
Could travel round the earth

Imagine how the world would be
If everyone could laugh
All the countries joining in
From Melbourne thro' to Bath.

So if you feel a smile begin
Don't leave it undetected
Let's start an epidemic quick
And get the world infected

Everybody needs to smile
It wipes away the pain
Just shout out hip hip hooray
And smile some more, again.

***Frank Harper***

## UNTITLED

A cry in the night
just another street fight
nobody cares anymore,
in the papers next day
hear the journalists say
another body found dead on the floor.

Life's gone wrong
people kill for a song
religion is often to blame,
black man or white
race shouldn't cause fights
the truth is we are all the same.

Whether Muslim or Jew
you're like me I'm like you
we should learn to love one another,
at the end of the day
prejudice gets in the way
turning love into hate for a brother.

Questions are many
answers ten for a penny
not all of them say the right things,
just live your life right
try to love not to fight
after all we're the same human beings.

***Chris Thomas***

## TREE

Your soul bared for all the world to see, twisted, gnarled,
An ugliness and yet a kind of beauty.
You spread your graceful branches to the air and say here I am,
This is me in all my glory.

Can I too bare my soul?
If I stand in your shadow and embrace you can I show the true me?
Shaded in your branches for ever to be rid of this veil of secrecy.

***Patricia Ann Evans***

## In A Good Way

You find it's your best aim, it might still be all the same,
you find it's your best way,
awoke on a Sunday, it might be a Monday,
go out on a good day.

*I saw a future erased, as I woke up instead,*
*past had chased it away, yet it's still in my head,*
*I sought what future today? As I woke up I lay,*
*it had changed yet again, but had stole all my friends.*

So now what do you say, hold on to the good days,
you'll find it's your best aim,
awake on a Sunday, OK so it's mundane
insight ain't a bad way.

***Stephen McMahon***

## LOVE FINDS A WAY

There sat an old woman alone in her chair
Not one passer-by had noticed her there
She looked in the mirror she held in her hand
No finer lass had there been in the land
She counted the wrinkles on her face she aspired
Each line brought a tear to her half seeing eyes
A hand on her shoulder and a gentle caress
Brought a smile to her face
As she came to rest
I'll remember the smile on her face each day
She went away happy
Because love found the way.

***Deena Teresa Howard***

## BUTTERFLY

Butterfly
Flutter by.
As I cry
River ripples glimmer;
In my eyes a shimmer.
Shiver
Quiver.
As the tear glistens
Butterfly
You listen.
Empty inside
We both hide
Behind fragile wings.
My heart sings.
Heart
Broken;
Unspoken.
Reeds wave.
A mind slave.
Crave
To fly,
Soar high
Like you.
Be free
Not me.
Flutter by
Butterfly.

***Amy Gillespie***

## To The Arum Lily

Of all the garden plants in summer
there isn't any other as pure white and pretty
than the tall arum lily.
Like sails of titanium white on light and strong verdian green
within its centre a cigar shaped stick of golden yellow
standing erect
to attract
spiders, bees and nightly moths
and when it rains
the water slides
inside the cuplike flower
resembling sails of olden ships.

The evening heralds the delicate perfume
waiting in each gentle breeze
how tall and graceful they stand at ease.
And on grey mornings they move quickly in the wind
like the huge hats of the sisters of St Vincent de Paul
as they go on their chores caring for the sick and the poor.

How large the leaves like huge hands saying please, please
we are also swaying in the breeze.
Of all the garden plants in summer
nothing can surpass the beauty of titanium white blooms
of the abundant arum lily.

***Raymond Spiteri***

## ECHOES

Echoes of silence resounded through depths of despair
wandering in time and space, knowing he isn't there
silence that fills me was once just an echoing roar
*silence* engulfs me where once I could see eagles soar.

Echoes of silence consume all my night and my day
a cavernous void of despair keeps my anger at bay
silence inside me destroys all the sounds that I love
and a screeching seagull which mimics the sound of a dove.

Echoes of silence compound as I lay on my bed
as love turns to hate with all these tears I have shed
echoes of laughter recede as silence invades
the dream is for real as reality silently fades.

Echoes of silence resounded through depths of despair
the sound of his voice which beckoned me into his lair
silence still fills me with sorrow and turbulent roar
my life is now nothing; once I would see eagles soar.

***Judy Studd***

## FACT AND FICTION

You can spend a hundred pounds
In a world that knows no bounds,
A day at the seaside, check out the zoo
Visit a town, see a country view.
If the chances were only a few,
'Love affairs', wait for you!
'Hit the town', have a Chinese meal
The best thing is it need not be real.

There's no such thing as wrong or right
As on a spaceship at dead of night
Give yourself a sci-fi fright!
No one asks why, the hours fly by
Horses gallop under a summer sky
Ghosts and ghouls, are also found
Haunted buildings, a ghostly hound
They live in a world devoid of sound
Altogether and neatly bound
Where can you find them? Where do we look?
The answer is easy, they're all in a book,
Better than this they all come free
Visit a library, you will see!

***Sheila Walters***

## SINCE WINE IS THE DRINK

Since wine is the drink for my wedding, serve on,
Fill my glass, let it run over and over,
Let me drink of it, for it is love.

Table, tables, many tables I have,
Bring the buckets, the big cold ones,
Now serve the wine from the coldest bottles.

Wine and dine me in the hall
Then wine and love me till the hours are small.

I'll drink on! Many bottles I drank,
Let me be merry, till the boys are up for a prank
Then give me more and more I say.

Since wine is the drink for my celebration drink on!
Share my wine and drink to my happiness
For I am in bliss and cannot be a miss.

***Dalsie Mullings-Powell***

# Age

Smiling eyes look up at my face,
Skin so fair but as rough as white lace,
Grey hair like cobwebs cover her frown,
As she dreams of the days where she'd be out around town,
She'd be dancing and free,
With many places still to see,
Dreaming of things that she could possibly be.

The photos that she keeps neatly away,
Remind her of her younger days,
Laughter, hard labour, children and more,
Everyone tells a story, right to the core.

Her delicate fingers curl around the cup like a cone,
Her hands all warm and worn feel like rough stone,
But never does she groan or moan.

Her smile is friendly,
The memory of it lasts forever,
Her mind still alert, proves she is still clever.

As I leave her home,
I turn to see,
Her silhouette in the distance waving at me.

***Hayley Fahey***

## For Old Times Sake!

Perfume, hair cream, oils and such
Itch reliever for the crutch
Breast implants to exaggerate
Lipstick, face paint to contemplate
Hot pants, T-shirt on which writing's seen
Fat reducers for the in-between
When a beauty one does invite
Into one's bed to spend the night
She could be, maybe what one needs
But what is hidden may make one freeze
Touch it, squeeze it until all's explained
That from the foregoing one has refrained
Ensure your sanctum remains secure
That you do not heartbreak endure
Or your ardour may then flop
As you watch your manhood drop
When she says that she loves you
And that she is a grandma too
That she does know others well
That she has a lot to sell
That's when you can reveal the truth
That you are no longer a youth
That you are a well made man
That her love is down the pan
That Viagra enhanced the fun
And that each the other has 'done'
Then you'd both laugh until your sides burst
Bragging that you came *to your senses first!*

***Jon El Wright***

## I LOVE YOU SHAMI

I love you, Shami, like there is no tomorrow. This love grows stronger each and every day. Never have I been struck so hard by love.

I love you with such an intensity that it hurts, but I will not stop loving you for as long as I have breath in my body.

My heart is overflowing with love, like a bath when the tap has been left running for too long.

I am like a schoolboy experiencing his first love and still get nervous before we meet.

Every time I see you my heart leaps and I need more oxygen because you take my breath away. One look and I am hypnotised, putty in your hands, open to any suggestion or instruction. Your hold over me is absolute.

I would do anything for you, whatever you asked, without question. That's love, a powerful emotion, perhaps the most powerful of all. Oh, my love, what power you possess.

I feel so deflated when we part, and wonder why time cannot stand still, to give us more time together, as long as we want.

Somehow, I get by when we are not together though with great difficulty.

But, each day we spend apart is one less day that we are together and that pains my heart.

I love you, Shami . . .

***Mark Pyne***

## I Am

I'm walking but I'm stumbling,
I'm talking but I'm slurred,
I'm thinking but my mind's blank,
I'm crying but there's no sound,
I'm sleeping but I'm awake,
I'm crazy but I'm sane!

***Reba Rajeda***

## TWILIGHT ANGEL

In the darkness of the night I dream of you
The closeness of your gentle body touches the inner reaches of my soul
I hear your voice so passionate whisper across the midnight breeze
I smell your perfumed top and close my eyes . . . picture you back
in my world
Where you once were . . . where you could have been . . .
where I still am . . .
Waiting for your love to reach out of the darkness and touch me again
We were like two ships that sailed through the dark oceans of life
But I did not want to leave the deep depths of your serene harbour
You were my twilight angel, a heavenly body of light through my
darkest times
As I still cling to the magic of you and what could have been
From my mind I cannot erase the beauty of your face from my dreams
Remember your body in my arms, cradling you until the
morning's dawn
I was stunned by your beauty and grace . . . your pure heart
Once there was a time in your life you were overshadowed by pain
I would listen, hold and caress you to help you feel again
But now you are back out there somewhere in the big wide world
I will not forget you my twilight angel, a lady who gave me so much
The memories of the times we walked, held hands and laughed
in the rain
Did not understand what pain was like until the day that you went away
I stand here alone, my head bowed in the darkness of the night, my
tears have run dry
Although your love still shines through to my heart like a beacon
of light
The memory of you lives on through my thoughts and dreams
How I desired the touch and feel of your warm body
Where in the throes of passion, and for that moment our two
bodies became one
Want to feel your tiny, fragile heart beating against my chest

I remember the feel of your touch well, it was as if time had stood still
Even though you have gone I cannot erase these memories of you
My heart will always be wrapped up in your warm smile and soft touch
To you I wave goodbye as I feel something in my heart begin to cry
I start to walk away from you my twilight angel, slowly disappearing into another life.

***Tony Puddifoot***

## The Needle Match

Next week the best will take the draft
And go away to war; the vital game is on,
The needle match when strategy
Is planned, the tactics tuned and honed,
Terrain discussed, the weather patterns
Read and understood, and somewhere
From past records old weaknesses exposed.

Early gains might soon be won; some losses
Inevitably sustained; but change of pace
Could well confuse once the big guns
Come in line and hold the southern front.
There'll be no quarter given, none returned,
The essence is attack, and not a hint
Of mercy mopping up the tail end slack.

Next week we'll unfurl banners, drink
A toast to victory, and celebrate the drafted
Best when they come marching home.

***Brian Parvin***

## WE MUST ALL TRY

My deepest emotions
Patient and virtuous
The outer shield protects my soul
Where my soft heart beats
Thriving on the energy which is love
Music of peaceful enmities
Harmonising through my veins
Every step taken in this world
Leaves behind the footsteps of hope
Like the symbol of love
The rose stands high, overflowing with beauty
Magnificent are the wonders of this world
Created for us by the hands of perfection
Never take anything for granted
Let us realise what we have, before it is lost
As the moon and the sun shares their light
Let us share the word of truth and right
Lonely is this Earth
Find the ally to your life
Fill the hollow cave in your spirit
You see you need love
Love is in our nature
Never be afraid to express passion
As love made the universe
It is our duty to keep it alive
Let us not be agitated
To decide what we feel
So our lives may be filled
With the happiness
In feeling what is real

***Marco Nigro***

## Building A City In My Room

Strike words into the ground.
Erect abstract bars from the paper horizon.
Pour concrete images into the framework.

Give the contents seven hours to condense.
Decorate the walls with metaphorical frescoes.
Open the front gate at dawn.

A delicate city rises in the morning light.
I'm writing down a hollow period.
A perfect one with its keyhole shape:
Through this hole
myriad eyes are peeking
In my city in my room.

I'd like to send my city to the transparent stomach of a bus,
to the colourful shoelaces of a newspaper or,
to the utopian living room of a book.

However my city has its own will, insisting to huddle up
in a crystal drop of rain above the vane,
relunctant to fall down.

***Chichi Lai***

## Fire And Water

Some say the world will end in fire,
Some say in water
From the destruction I've tasted
Of uncontrolled desire
I hold with those who favour fire.

But if it had to perish twice
I think I know enough of hatred
To liken it to water turned ice
It is also great
And would suffice.

***Mary Cathleen Brown***

## SOLVENTS SOLVE

Solvents . . . sold
To me, to you
Do solvents solve?
Perhaps they do
The fumes enfold
Sensations new
So new, so true and yet so old
Do solvents solve?
Not so, I'm told:
The chilling queue of bodies rolled
In sheets anew, who thought so too
Were overbold, inhaled the glue:
Their bodies crumple, fall and fold
My friends . . . Gary, Jason, Lou,
Their souls departed (but . . . where to?)
So . . .
Do solvents solve?
No.
But . . .
Addiction holds
Ensnares, controls
Dissolves a hole within your soul . . .
The cap pops off, the scent of glue
Helpless now, inhale . . . and problems solved.
Sensations old - solvents *do* solve!
But . . .
Sensation new
I'm falling, into shadowed hue
So blue . . .
So cold . . .

***Terry Dutton***

## Me And Myself In A Room Isolated

He is alone among thousands
I am accompanied among none
Me and myself in a room isolated.

In my world I wish, I seek
In my world I conceive, I receive
Me and myself in a room isolated.

My heart wishes, my mind furnishes,
My soul rejoices, nourished
Me and myself in a room isolated.

He says, 'I can't.' I say, 'I can.'
He asks, 'How?' I say, 'When?'
Me and myself in a room isolated.

My world is so pure, free from deception
I am the king of mine
He is slave of his.

Me and myself in a room isolated.

***Syed Jilani***

## BULLY OFF

Why do you bully me?
The small child said.
Is it just for fun, does
What you do give you street cred?

I'm so small
You're tall and big,
Why do you push,
Poke and dig?

Have I hurt you,
Upset you some way?
You only have to tell me,
You only have to say.

I'm sorry my presence
Causes you distress
I'm lost for words
My faults please express.

Has someone else hurt you?
You should tell your dad or mom
Then p'raps we'd all know
Where the anger's coming from.

It's not fair to pick
On me and others
I've no friends
Or big brothers.

I could be your friend
You could be mine
We could be good buddies
Yes, we could given time.

It takes more strength to be good
Than to be bad all the time
We'll share my lunch box
Take two sandwiches, that's fine.

***Ann Weavers***

## DOREEN

*(Dedicated to my grandmother the poet)*

Crags and trickles cracked through her time
Her thoughts composed in rhythms and rhyme
She is all ages when writing a line
All her memories are then mine
The crags are now real
And the trickles go to sea
The view is a circle
A dream now reality
Crystal perception
Meditation to pen
Pen to paper
And not much later
A snap shot in life
Eternalised by the translator

***Leah Sadler***

## PATHWAY

Stones obstructing,
Ancient ways,
Misty distance,
By resistance.

Blocking the path,
Between the trees,
Yet memory,
Has insistence.

Then turning back,
To wilderness,
In solitude,
With vague unease.

A right of way,
Denied, still waits,
Quietly for,
Fair persistence.

For it was here,
Before this day,
Existed, yes,
Before this time.

Was of this earth,
With sandstone rock,
Past, present and
Yet future time.

***Kathleen M Scatchard***

## ADULTS VS KIDS

Kids are taken for granted,
Not to be seen and not even heard!
We're meant to live our daily lives,
Without even saying a word!

Now why can't you sit there nicely
Like I always used to do?
Feet off the chairs, tidy your room,
Keep your mouth shut whilst you chew.

Oh, Mum why do we have to do homework?
It's the most painful job on Earth.
Try cooking, washing and ironing
And have you ever given birth?

They tell us off for moaning,
But what else shall we do with our day?
We go to school - what a waste of time,
Then there's not enough time to play.

And finally we come to music,
Modern, hip-hop style.
But they still interrupt - get that rubbish off,
I'm gonna listen to classical for a while.

So my conclusion to this poem,
Parents - who needs 'em, eh?
We get pushed around, day and night,
Can't you at least let us have our say?

***Kirsty Thompson (13)***

## Sleep

Sleep eludes me.
Longing to nestle in the soft wool,
I stare at the pattern.

I cast on, trying to empty my mind
Of all but the smooth passing of the wool
Around the steadily interweaving needles.

At the end of each short row I shuffle and turn.
The needles click irritatingly, stabbing behind my lids.
Knit one, purl one, knit one, purl . . .

One stitch drops down the rows.
As the pattern unravels I chase it back
Through yesterday, tomorrow, next year.

All night the pattern grows in fits and starts.
At six I wake and dress,
The garment misshapen, itchy, tight.

***Caroline Smith***

## ONE

One vision shared by us all
One friend in case we should fall
One voice to lead the way
One prayer will save the day
One desire a world without strife
One path the highway of life
One hope a road that is clear
One faith and we no longer fear
One word can be misunderstood
One pride but it does us no good
One trust if we could but perceive
One truth if we'd only believe
One anger the cowards way out
One joy makes us all want to shout
One song if we all sing in tune
One love let it come to us soon
One tear and the world starts to cry
One goal let it not pass us by
One smile such joy it would bring
One stable was fit for a king
One light our star will now shine
One forgiveness there still is the time
One belief the fighting to cease
One dream a world blessed with peace

***A Mitchell***

## GET A LOAD OF THIS (GOD BLESS J K ROWLING)

What woman is this
Without a home and a kiss?
In Bristol Park the nights so lonely and cold,
In Gardener's Crescent the manuscript but keeping her bold,
Where ignorance is bliss isn't it folly to be wise?
Harry Potter manuscript rejected like a useless piece,
J K Rowling's booed just like Jesus by the Pharisees,
Her manuscript a parable only understood by a few,
They have got eyes but they don't see,
They have got ears but they don't hear,
Bloomsbury the good Samaritan where
She finally saw light and day.

***Cuthbert Makwetura***

## NOON IN SPACESHIPS ACROSS THE UNIVERSE

Of my troubled sleep
And abstract nightmares
Where death will claim
Us all

Take a stranger's pain
Tell them your name
See the face change
To smile.

Alien artefacts
On crusty road surface
Baked by sunbeams
Caught in dumb eyes that pry.

Ahoy! me boy.
And girls,
From times past, present and future,
Warping time to suit the hour
Of your need, indeed!
What rot!

Me thinks me smell a rat
Somewhere within your baking heart
Caught in a crossfire of soul bullets that spray
*Rat-a-tat-tat!*

Never hitting the visible,
Only the invisible targets your blind eyes see
All too readily accepting the impossible over the possible.

Fool lies prostrate on the universe's edge
Bloodshot eyes wide in wonder and fear
Is that God in Heaven singing His own praises
Or the Devil in Hell fooling me again?

The spaceship hums above me,
Calls me towards its oval doors of light.
I see voices in faces.
Strange as it seems, I have dreamt of my death
Whilst dying alone on the inside
But never out
Never visible
To you.

Zooming through the unchartered
Drinking tea, eating cake
Was the life I chose so
Safe,
Bland
And pain free?

Give me a sword that I may throw myself upon it
Feel the blade
Slice through
This horror.
Oh God, why me?
I am the lost sheep.

The noise has stopped
And I am still
This is the end
The doors open silently
There is no light
Only dark stars in a colourless sky
And now I can see no more.

***Stephen Power***

## THE JOURNEY

The journey has been dark,
Supernovas were dim and fleeting.
Cherubs fell like apples and
Hope died in its cage.

Lying, head caressed by pillow,
Upon the rusty berth
Spirit bleached and withered
Tormented by the earth.

The spectral curtains haunt the piety
The wind chime chants a ghostly tune
Serenading the part of me held hostage
By the impending sense of doom.

The lantern fades, fingers
Like branches, torn from bark
Supernovas did not inspire,
The journey has been dark.

***Tim Coles***

## TICKY'S 50TH BIRTHDAY

Ticky is the one who has the shiny bald head.
He also has a belly, which looks well fed.
He has a cheeky smile hid behind his 'tache,
I think he's quite well off, with lots of lovely cash.

He is our local plumber, he will fix your blocked loo,
Your leaky pipes and lots more too.
A few weeks he may take to call, it could be two or three,
But when he comes a-calling, he will say, 'Where's the tea?'

He taps you on the arm when he's got something to say,
He points and stares and looks around, that's just his little way.

But there's nothing we would change about this chap called Tic,
Of all the mates there are, he's the one to pick.
Have a great 50th birthday Tic, and a very good weekend.
Lots of love and all the best from Vin, your old friend.

***Lavinia S Townsend***

## TEXTURE

Imagine every emotion you ever felt
had a different texture,
that you could touch and learn,
either pleasing or concerning
the nature of discomfort,
found in feeling something confusing
or else found in feeling something alluring.

And would feeling, by finger, lend answer?

And would feeling by hand
make the hurt understand –
love is real?

***John Scott McLachlan***

## UNTITLED

The angry sea, so cold and grey,
Hurls its strength at the rocks,
Wearing, tearing their beauty away,
Once alive with seabirds in flocks.
Nature is bad.
The sky so full of ugly clouds,
Fighting and squabbling there,
They cover the earth like shrouds,
To go, not knowing where.
Nature is wild.
The wind that cries in hopefulness,
Not knowing what to find,
The rain that answers in tearfulness,
Washing out the mind.
Nature is sad.
The sun comes out to shine,
The sea is calm and friendly,
The sky is blue, birds hover a while,
The earth is now so heavenly.
Nature is good.

***Lynne Law***

## UNFINISHED

Bring me the heads
Of dead roses.
Bring me dried violets.

Put nails through
The eyes of the people.

What you don't know can't hurt.

Bring me bandaged ladies
And their dying babies.
I will wallow in this.

If I catch my breath
(On wings)
I will allow a whisper
To escape my broken lips.

Words wrapping round;
Your deep throat
Vibrating as you scream.
Everything will make sense

In death;
In this.

This is a dead state,
A blank card,
A fool's device
That will never become a reality,
Remaining locked within a vision.
A falsitude faltering.

Stab my praying hands.
Because I wanted you.

Unfinished business
I meant to finish,
But I am not enamoured by change.
I want you to stay.

I helped unstable bonds to break.
Because I wanted you.

I am the stain
That will not fade;
The king
Who refuses to abdicate.

I am poison
In your bloodstream.
You are disease.

A sweet virus.

A caring death.
A desired flu.

A toxic heart dealer,
I will sell sex at the side of the road
To charge my ventricles
If for only an hour.

Each blue kiss,
Each sedative;
It helps me get over you.

A cross to hang upon,
A noose to dangle from.
I drown into myself
And I fold like water lilies in a monsoon.

With only the moon to tell
Of how I crave your morphine.

Anaemic with drugs
I am a bone structure,
A marrow grenade;
Please pull the pin from my mouth.

Because I wanted you.

***Ben McClure***

## Days

Time has shifted, and nothing could be done,
too fast to catch the glimpses of those wasted hours.
Those days that slip like butter from the lip,
and in weight they are a tonne.

Slipping and sliding, days become years,
they multiply and then you die.
Hours are short, don't waste them, don't blink! don't think!
Don't cry.

***Aleksandra Bullock***

## SPOOKY GOINGS ON

'What's that noise? Did you hear that?'
'It's just the mewing of a cat.'
'A cat that snarls with a tiger's roar?'
'It's just a cat and nothing more.'
'There's something there, of that I swear.'
'Then take a look, of that I dare.'
'I'd rather stay in bed and hide.'
'Maybe it's a ghost that lurks outside?'
'Oh, stop it now, you're being ghoulish.'
'And you, my dear, are being foolish.'
'There's a fiend outside our door, it's true.'
'It's not me it's after, dear one, it's you.'
'Oh, don't say that! I'm so afraid.'
'Its devilish plan you can't evade.'
'Stop it now, I'm very scared.'
'To meet with fate you must be prepared.'
'There! The noise once more, you surely heard?'
'Indeed! Something in the night has stirred.'
'Oh gosh, what is it? What ever can it be?'

'Do you not hear me knocking? I forgot my key!'

***C Ridgway***

## Words To Mark

For all the times you hurt me,
You must know I'm hurting still.
Each day I'm thinking of you
As I take my bitter pill.

For all the times you let me down,
The days I wait in vain,
You know I'm waiting here for you
And I'll take you back again.

***Sue Corbin***

## Who Do I See?

I look into my mirror, a girl stares,
She has long curly hair.
There is no smile upon her face,
She looks so lonely, so out of place,
I give her a smile, her eyes shine.
She places her hand into mine.
Images of her life flash before my eyes,
I feel my tears, from my eyes I cry.
I can see her mum and dad.
Fighting constantly, she's so sad.
She blames herself for all their tears,
I can feel her suffering over many years.
I see another flash before my eyes.
Many men have come and gone from her life.
Cheats, liars and abusers, more that I can't say,
I'm feeling the hurt. Why did they treat her this way?
Another flash, she's being sick,
Bulimic I think is the name for this,
She lost control, wanted to die,
Again the tears fall from my eyes.
Now I see a knife cutting deep,
She's trying hard to make blood seep.
I can see she has succeeded but people soon are there,
I'm guessing these are people that truly care.
Another flash full of pills,
Antidepressants, her pain I can feel.
Tried to overdose, didn't succeed,
Her body too weak. She wants to be free.
Another appears, a baby I see,
She has a daughter, someone she needs.
I feel their bond, I feel their love,

I feel bad fortune has given up.
                    No more flashes, I'm in reality,
Only to find that little girl was me.
How my life was such a mess,
Now I have my little girl, I am truly blessed.

***Sonia Schollar***

## TEARS

Tears, good tears,
Tears of happiness,
Tears of joy,
Tears of heavy or light relief,
Tears of true, such true belief.

Tears, bad tears,
Tears of anger, hurt and pain,
Tears of a future lost or a tainted past,
Tears whose pain will forever last.

Tears, just tears,
Tears for those who lived before they died,
Tears for life - because it's good and bad,
Luxury tears, that come and go,
Tears for that poor old so and so.

Tears, no tears,
The tears that you never cried,
The tears just left inside.
These are tears that won't just go away,
Tears that are never wept, every day.

So sob my friends and let it be,
Sob for breakfast,
Sob with tea,
Whether your tears be loud or dry,
Sometimes we all need to stop and cry.

***Jake Hayman***

## Lost

As I walked into the night
I still carried the heavy load,
The load that was placed on my proud shoulders;
Tear of old crimson marks from an age ago
Archaic in its shimmering hidden form
Slaking like the hungry wolf.

As the moon dips her head to take a better look,
Watching me for my next move; eyes wide!
As I ponder on my desertion from my truth,
The heavy clouds glide past and shut out the shadows
And all that's left is a lonely man with a heart of gold.

***Ricky N Lock***

## YOUR LOVE MY LOVE

Lovely flowers, happy hours
That's just what our love means
You beside me there to guide me
Your love is the answer to my dreams

When I first met you it was love right from the start
For love like ours will stay deep in my heart
Please let me prove just how I feel
As time goes by I will love you still

Life can be happy, life can be sad
But with you beside, good times we'll have
Don't ever leave me because I need you so
Being with you gives me a loving glow

I will always be with you, come what may
Always, always, not for just a day
Give me your love and I will give you mine
Tell me our love will last to the end of time

Lovely flowers, happy hours
That's just what our love means
You beside me there to guide me
Your love is the answer to my dreams.

***G R Breakspear***

## SEPARATE

He stopped loving me the other day
Hasn't told me yet, doesn't need to say
Doesn't miss me like he used to do
Can't remember the last time he said, 'I love you'
The look in his eyes has gone, disappeared
I knew it would happen, it's what I feared
The conversation is gone, talk has run dry
So why won't he end it, just let it die?
He doesn't feel the same anymore, so what is the use?
I'd rather he set me free, just cut me loose
Doesn't touch me like he used to, can't stand the sight
I don't know what has changed, can't make it right
Love him to pieces, but it's fallen apart
His mind has moved on, no longer have his heart
It saddens me to think we are going to separate
But he's not happy, I suppose it's fate
I mess most things in my life up
No surprise to me, though quite abrupt
I'll move on again I suppose; well I hope
Like always I'm sure I'll be able to cope.

***Charlotte Watkins***

## SENSING YOU

Sometimes just
the slightest draught
caresses my skin,
or perhaps a familiar scent
tickles my nose.
Another time I think
I hear you laugh.
A light tinkling . . .
So my heart lifts,
content, to believe
the spirit goes
forever, into eternity.

***V M McKinley***

## HIGH STREET ADVENTURE

It's many years ago now but I remember still
Of a time when I was young, I think I always will
When three of us teenagers were strolling through the town
Without a care and laughing as we were walking down
Towards the local golf course for a few friendly rounds
On that lovely day in June with all the summer's sounds
Suddenly a policeman appeared before our eyes
Held up his hand stopping us, greatly to our surprise
'Can you spare a half hour, lads?' he asked in a kindly tone
'Down at the police station, it should not take too long'
So we accompanied him and met there many more
Soon we were placed in line wondering what's in store
A prisoner was brought out and placed in the line
Two policemen then led out a young girl bearing signs
Of having been badly beaten up, her eyes were shiny black
The three went down the line and slowly walked back
On the return she stopped, near to me she placed
Her hand on the shoulder of the next man she faced
In distress she was led away, they also took the man
They thanked us for our time, shook our hands, then we ran
Outside the sun was shining and our fears began to fade
But I will never forget that identity parade.

***T Daley***

## I Am

I am, the speck of dust, the grain of rust,
The sand beneath your feet.
I am, the leaves that rustle, the hustle bustle,
The eyes of those you meet.

A cloud am I, that floats on high,
The sun that burns your skin.
I am the moon, I watch you sleep,
I am your soul within.

The wisp of hair, caressing there,
Are whispered words from me.
I am the longest day you've known,
I am eternity.

I am a place, I'm every face,
That gives a knowing look.
I am each bird, that flies unheard,
I'm words in every book.

I am your sky, as you walk by,
On eagle's wings I soar.
I'm every breath you breathe my love,
Until you're home once more.

***N P Brogan***

## Love To Un-Love

Why is it when they want to end it,
they always say, 'It's not you - it's me!'
When what they really mean is,
'It's not you stopped loving me - it's me stopped loving you!'

When it used to, always just be 'us' . . .

Then they follow up with the classic,
'I need some space!'
When in reality, what' they're really saying is,
'Actually, you're in my way!'

When space needed was once room inside of me . . .

Followed by that old familiar chestnut,
'We can still be friends -
(but just not with each other!)'

When you'd always vowed true friendship based on forever . . .

In the beginning, those three simple words,
'I love you!'
So shouldn't an ending be condensed into one small word?
'Goodbye!' - Simple as that.

***Sally Barker***

## You Can Look Outside But Maybe It Is Being Where You Are

I have been wise and I
Have been young,
Sometimes I don't think
I have learnt a thing.

I know every word
In the song,
If you want to cheat,
You have to wake up early
To catch me out.

You can look outside for happiness
Or whatever you find close,
But maybe it's being
Where you are.

It is happy when you first meet
But sad when the person has gone,
Just remember it is all
Part of the fun.

I have chased many a rainbow
On many a silver lining.
They may have tried to hurt me,
But none of them have got me.

Don't be afraid to stand in front of love
If you can't go for what you want,
Then who is to blame?

You can look outside for happiness
Or whatever you find close,
But it's not the same as
Being where you are.

***Diane Mangal***

## TRUST

divine divinity
can U feel it?
U're not free
if U can't.

experience life
know Love,
it's everywhere.
U're not free
if U don't.

U are divine,
I am divine,
remember.
U're not free
if U won't.

do
experience
do
what U wish.
harm none, let it be done.

please yourself,
trust yourself,
please trust yourself
instinctively.
U'll be free.

the Sun is shining,
the stars are out,
this must be
what Love's about.

***Ashley Tame***

## Blame It All On Mankind

The human race is on the verge of extinction
Total obliteration with no colour or race distinction
This is the work of modern man in self-destruction
Through rigidity in accepting criticism and correction
And total failure to bring reasonable re-construction
Mankind has gone too far without divine intervention

At this rate mankind is walking a tightrope
Warring parties leave us with no string of hope
Lives are being destroyed by genocide acts
Tribe perish under dirty works of pseudo cults
And many are victims of deadly suicidal attacks
Mankind will vanish and leave no marks

Ozone depletion will not sustain life on this world
Pollution being emitted into space is now threefold
Effluent discharge has left marine life in the cold
Destruction of fauna and flora has left a story untold
And the greenhouse effect long started to unfold
Mankind is digging own grave in search for the odd

Hunger and disease have sent lives down the drain
Most of the dead are retired and helpless children
Restoration of hope for these lives is like a pipe dream
We stand and watch lives vaporise into air like steam
And as the victim figures begin by each day to soar
Mankind is quick to record statistics albeit gore

At this rate mankind is on board a sinking ship
The cutting edge of accidents has not missed a step
Carnage on the roads has gone wild as we all know
Capsizing ships are yet another inevitable blow
And light accidents end up in an unavoidable glow
Mankind is queuing on a chainsaw-massacre show.

***Everson Mpofu***

## CHEDWORTH

It's a secluded spot.

And you can almost see him linger there,
The wealthy Roman, noble, dignified;
Standing beside the open villa door
Breathing the peace of open countryside;
Assured, as the Cotswolds' gentle twilight falls,
That all is well within those sheltering walls.

It is quiet there.

And you can almost hear the sandalled feet
Advancing over worn mosaic floor;
And catch the unfamiliar shouts that greet
A father just returned - perhaps from war;
And maybe from a cool and inner room,
The strains of lutes played softly through the gloom.

But it's a remote spot too.

And were they content, I wonder, just to be
Living by English fields and rills;
Or did they yearn for far off Italy
And the great city, built on seven hills?
Did Roman blood beat strongly in their veins
Or did they find delight in English lanes?

***Muriel Rawson***

## EMPTY BOTTLES

I
stand
on
a
piece
of
ground
where they say you are buried
no
head
stone
no
to
my
*Dad*
wreath
upon
your grave
nothing to show you existed
only me and your empty bottles.

***Martina Quirke***

## TOXIC CHEMICALS

Up above the sound of heavy machines rolls on
Through the night and through the day,
Spraying their toxic chemicals come what may.

Hark! Do not stir or make a sound
As man with his sticks of fire
Will bring death to us all with his cans of death,
And his relentless hound.

Hush! All has gone quiet and still,
Do we make dash for it over the nearest hill?
Quick! Run as fast as you can,
Before nature's worst enemy catches us.
He's called 'man'.

***A J Price***

## PATIENCE, PATIENT

I've cried, I've wept whilst carers slept
I feel I'm left alone
And would infer they are inept
So I've got cause to moan.

A corridor was all I had
While waiting for a pill
The stay I had just made me mad
So should I write my will?

At last a bed, plenty of air
I couldn't reach my pot
The nurses don't consider care
I sobbed, is that my lot?

Same patient in a different guise
And different set of rules
A word unto the very wise
The staff are not just fools.

I slept, was seen by doctors two
'Tis best to stay laid out
A ward when ready, that's their view
Of that there is no doubt.

Door ajar is what's been ordered
The pot put out of sight
Muscle freedom can't be hoarded
To help me in my plight.

At last I'm home and fit again
My body as before
The NHS can deal with pain
We could not ask for more.

***J Kay***

## Night Clouds

The white mares of the moon rush along the misty sky
Beating their golden hooves upon the glass heavens;
The white mares of the moon are all standing on their hind legs
Pawing at the green porcelain of the remote heavens.
Fly, mares!
Strain your utmost,
Scatter the milky dust of stars,
Or the tiger sun will leap upon you and destroy you
With one lick of his vermilion tongue.

***Ammar Kalia (10)***

## A STRANGER IN HIS OWN LIVING ROOM

I remember when we first met -
a blind date I almost chickened out of
a few beers - you looking like 'medallion man',
me being all upfront blasé and just being myself.

But still we wanted to see each other again -
no sweat, no airs and graces, no hassle
just a comfortable ease and lots of laughter.
You were just like me - I was like you -
we thought alike, we looked alike
and I felt like I'd come home at last.

We took the chance - meeting twice a week,
which soon turned to all day, every day
and suddenly I quite liked this.
In the past, I'd normally have run a mile.

You even told me you loved me,
swore we'd always be best friends
and we hadn't even s****** together.
For once I didn't feel like running - I didn't even want to.

Sitting on your mum's settee,
stroking tenderly the inside of my elbow
an erogenous zone I didn't even know I had!
You were me, I was you - and suddenly, naturally,
We were in harmony, alone - together.

This was it! After 34 years I'd finally found 'the one'
and for six years we were happy -
For six glorious years, we fought, we laughed and we cried.
But always together.

Until the seventh year, I came home to find
a stranger sitting in his own living room
and I couldn't reach him -
I couldn't even begin to touch the surface,
I didn't know how.

Suddenly our erogenous zones were no longer important
we didn't even know how to fight together anymore -
so I did my crying alone.
We couldn't laugh - there was nothing to laugh at.

And so you moved on - the Stranger
and after seven years the you and I that were
became the 'us' that will never be
so now I'm resigned to crying alone -
but guaranteed I'll be laughing again soon
But neither will ever be with you again.

***Sally Barker***

## Oh To Be Old

So I've been told that when you get old
Your hair turns curly and grey,
Your feet buckle in and your legs buckle out
And your speech kind of whittles away.
So I've been told that when you get old
Your gnashers stop gnoshing the food,
Your fingers they fight in the still of the night
And your legs just don't know what to do.
Your stomach it grumbles to the sound of your mumbles
And your eyes can't stop staring the room,
Your knees crick! And crunch! As you hear yourself munch
Upon all that sloshy baby food.
Oh to be old, I can't wait as I'm told
All the good things that happen to me.
I am getting older but for now I'll be bolder
And just stay at sweet thirty-three.

***Becky Royce***

## Thank You

Thank you for the diamonds that twinkle in the sky,
And the emerald grass and trees
That are pleasing to the eye.
Thank you for the rubies in the setting sun.
Thank you for the aquamarine of a dawn begun.
If you look keenly it is easy to see
All the jewels of the earth that you have given me,
Amethyst in the flower violet,
Sapphires in the sky,
Jade in a green sea,
Don't let any pass you by.
I don't need any precious stones,
They aren't necessary for me,
Because thank you, Lord Jesus,
I have them all completely for free.
I only have to look with my eyes,
Another precious gift you gave to me.

***Pat Todd***

## Newborn

The sweat and labour done
Here you lie, sweet child
Enclosed in my arms.
Never will I forget this moment.
I hold you against my heart,
Your long, thin, mottled limbs
Snugly wrapped
Still seem part of me
Enclosed in my arms.
My lips trace the down-covered
Perfection of your head,
Feel the pulse at temple and crown
And am overwhelmed
At your vulnerability
Eyes tight shut, a frown at your brow
The windows of your soul are closed
Not yet ready to face this world.
Of what do you dream
As movements flicker beneath your eyelids?
Suddenly your eyes are open
Porcelain and palest blue
They gaze unflinchingly into mine
And I am lost in love and wonder.

***Mary Daulton***

## CASTING EYES

A dark change is coming, I can feel it,
My destiny has changed, shifted from light to dark.
I don't understand what's going on.
Why do these feelings come to me?
This is not who I'm supposed to be,
People looking at me the wrong way, judging me.
Why do they think they have the right?
I've seen him looking more closely recently,
I guess he's trying to figure me out.
These mixed up signals buzzing around me,
Changing my shape constantly,
Even I can't keep up.
He's always staring, always looking,
Documenting my life.
Why am I so appealing to him?
I'm nothing special, but I know he must see something,
Or why does he look?
Maybe he'll come close enough to tell me why?

***Dylan Angel Halliwell***

## SUNDAY, 4.30

With my hands in the washing-up bowl,
I hear the poet's words
warmly drip.
He pronounces;
each, pause, perfect,
turning his tongue
as my sponge
scours cups.
Each syllable sounded
like a struck glass
chime
and by the time
the plug is pulled,
the words swirl
and slip away.
Damp handed,
I blotch paper
to try to write,
before
it drains.
My biro,
waiting,
warmly drips.

***Damyon Hardy***

## There Was Once Chance

There was once chance
Which shone my way;
The light was bright,
But not of day.
The spark remaining in my heart,
Broke through
To pick the lucky card.
Who knew,
The chance was facing right,
To see me
Holding my head high;
The pride was winning
My heart over,
Neglected feelings,
Drowning lower.

There was once chance,
But that day's gone;
The sorry feeling
Holding on.
The luck was knocking on my door,
With cracking walls
And squeaking floor.
I welcomed Mother -
Happy glow,
To find her holding
Wise head low.
This was a sorry sign for me,
When chance was mine,
I let it flee.

***Sofia Pernikis***

## THE MOBILE MENACE

The whole world's gone quite crazy, everyone's got mobile phones,
it seems they're very handy, that they cross all known time zones.
It's said they aid the user and they do it seems amuse,
though why this is I cannot say, for frankly I'm confused.
All my family have one, they tell me that it's great,
and that I need to calm right down and not get in a state.
It must be this new language, talk of SIM cards and of text
that really gets me quite wound up and very, very vexed.
There's often non to answer when I try to make a call,
and all this talk of voice mail has me driven up the wall.
When nobody has answered and I mention it or moan,
I'm often told the reason is, they've left the phone at home.
And even more upsetting and I really get irate,
is when they haven't heard it ring because it's on vibrate.
Technology is so advanced the things can now take pictures,
they send out tunes and kids play games that have them all in stitches.
Everyone is quite convinced that mobiles are a ball,
wouldn't it be super if they used the thing to simply make a call?
When the monster's left at home, in the car or on a train,
even really clever folk forget they have a brain.
They really start to panic asking, 'What am I to do?'
dashing all around the place, getting in a stew.
As if without their mobiles they will be in dire straits,
left bereft it's just as if they can't communicate.
Surely modern science was intended for the best,
but all these flaming mobiles cause a great deal of unrest.
It may be I'm old fashioned, out of date, or simply scared,
or maybe I'm just happy folks, to be a techno nerd.

***Mo Fletcher***

## THE SEA

The sea.
Where lives are lost
And hearts are broken.
The sea.
A place of peace,
Tranquillity, serenity,
Ferocity!
The sea.
The dreams I have dream back to me
Reflection, blueness, calmness, still
The one I love,
The sea.

***C S Hindshaw***

## Laura – Behold The Light That Shines In My Eyes Today

Laura Marie Goatcher, your name will always be
Though your maiden name will fade as time goes on
But these are the days upon which I'll fondly gaze
For I know in my mind's eye, how swift they'll be gone.

As often as I can I'll share sunshine and laughter
I'll be there to share in your tears in more shadowy times
But I always will be here to bring you some wisdom
To give your thoughts some reason, when nothing rhymes.

You are my second grandchild, but my first little girl
The image of how your mother was years ago
But her dark hair and eyes are replaced with yours so fair and blue
And I will relive all those memories, watching you grow.

Already your first words have brought me joy beyond compare
Observed by one who is older, wiser-eyed
Bidding me guide and lead you gently down life's magic road
So making your wish come true with every stride.

When you can understand my words, you'll know you have it all
Within your own grasp to overcome any obstacle,
One step at a time, and with courage at your heels
Of your own convictions, setting all your own ideals.

When your brother Jack was born, my role in life moved on
And I learned how to let time stand perfectly still
So life could then be seen in a strangely different light
I could train my mind to see clearly, by power of will.

Time to think for you will not be so easy
You will always want to run when you should walk
Your view of the pace of life will only be seen with eyes of the young
In your mind you will only hear voices of youthful talk.

Fulfilling our dreams would be easy, if only we would from the start
Follow the signs that our own selves give us,
On the way to a happy heart
Those inner 'feelings' that the road ahead is the right inclination,
Or too high
Is something deep inside that no one else can 'feel' or 'hear'
Or even pry.

Listen to those whispers, for they will provide the key
To the doors that reveal your own self - your heart and soul
Inspiration will be waiting when you slowly turn that key
And unlock the secret store of your own wishes,
You'll perceive your goal

My one wish for you would be simple -
That you don't take too long to unearth
Your own secret longings, but, above all that -
The value of your own true worth
For knowing yourself is the one attribution that many take
A lifetime to possess
But, without such a wealth of information -
You will never understand true happiness.

***Grandad David F Marsh***

## A Beautiful Place

I can't wake up any more,
But my eyes are open wide
To see the world
that makes me tremble in fear . . .

Like a lost child, I stand
To find the one thing
No one could ever find.

In my deepest dreams and desire
It became a nightmare of reality . . .
On what rock should I stand
To weigh my faith of the world
I have endured for so long?

I look backwards with my face forward
To see the hunting tigers of the past . . .

Whom should I hold on to?
I thought it was you,
But you were the past I hid from . . .

But where should I look?
There is no more to do . . .
In this thing I will call a place,
I think I will just wait . . .

In an invisible touch
I have foreseen a beautiful place,
Where there is no quake,
And a golden calabash that will never break.

***Omolei Asikhia***

## THE DESTRUCTION OF BAGHDAD CITY

O Saddam, Saddam
You have been warned
O Saddam, Saddam
It is a pity
That we had to go to war
All your tanks, guns and bombs
We shall destroy them
We will!
All the people of Baghdad
Are mourning for their dead
O Baghdad, Baghdad
It is a pity
That we had to go to war
To the north west
Lies Baghdad city
Dawn and grey sunset
Dark cloud
Sadness and misery
Everywhere!
O Baghdad, Baghdad
It is a pity
That we had to go to war!

***P B James***

## Loneliness

About the ninth hour
From the cross
From the heart of Jesus
Came a loud cry
A cry that echoed down the years

Eloi; Eloi, Lama Sabachtani

My God, my God, why has thou
Forsaken me?
A cry
That sympathised
With
The depressed; the abandoned; the forlorn; and the lonely
The widow; the widower; the orphaned; the hungry;
The outcast; the half-caste; those degraded by war
Cast off by society; the downcast; the poor.

To all
Who received Him
Who believed in His name
He gave power to become children of God
Who were born
Not of the flesh and blood of man
But by the Spirit of God
'Call on Him now.'

***Patrick McCarthy***

## THE TIMEKEEPER

My love, beneath the clouds run deep, colourful veins of our lives
Minutes, hours, days, asleep we count the stars tonight
To so reflect, not to reject our inherited imperfections
Open wounds left unattended to bleed our identities dry
Thy kindest hearts suffering at ye hands of duty no more
The chase of time no longer bearing down on us
Have no need to fear your infectious temper
The clock, its chime is heard, yet left to go unnoticed here
Fatal in her grasping claw we watched the fragile threads of life
Sustain thy beating heart no more - daughter, lover, mother,
sister, wife
Go without hesitation then, she will be there in her endless beauty
No wonder then, the mistress comes and seeks to reaffirm her position
Weaving her poison beneath our delicate skin
She leaves us breathless, motionless, parallel in this universe
Protecting herself with her heart veneered with enamel
Leaving no thought in the labyrinth of her mind for us
Words spoken on well-worn paths of our beginnings
Will remain locked between our eternal souls
Endorsing my love for you even more
Cherish the times, cherish the moments
Once gone can never be returned
Only in our minds, our hearts, our beginnings and our end.

***Jacqueline Taylor***

## Chardin's Still Life With Game

At first glance, it would appear
As though, in slumber they do sleep;
Entangled in dreams of Eden, two buff
Hares, caressed by pheasant's rustic

Hues. Not far from the intimacy of the
Three, an apple sits apart; partially
Hidden from the scene by a veil of
Mottled curling leaf. Looking away from

The sunken eyes of hapless beasts, into
The mad, bewildered eye of stricken bird,
Screaming from within (it may seem)
A narcoleptic sleep; neck limp, hanging.

From light-emitting ledge the tempting
Flesh of fruit that lies beneath a yellowed
Skin, teases towards the fertile eye
Of the captivated voyeur's mind.

The serpent shadow slithers, on the ochre wall.

***J Spiers***

## WHY?

War is escalating in Iraq and Afghanistan
Bombs, landmines and gunfire in Palestine
Clashes of religion in Northern Ireland
Killing, fighting in the whole land
Why?

I am working far away from home
Far from my family, to earn a bit more
While others are living in extravagance
Spending all their quids on booze and cracks
Why?

He has a mansion, they have huts
She eats caviar, I'm satisfied with rice
Her car is a limo, they travel on a cab
Party is their life, while we're stuck on our jobs.
Why?

I am sick and tired of always asking
Why everything on earth is not the same
There are wealthy and there are poor
Terrorism, disputes, famine and war.
Why?

Why suffering and destruction?
Why hatred, vengeance and opposition?
What are the roots of all these pains?
There is only one answer, but we are to blame.

***Lee N Fausto***

## FORGOTTEN

The wind is bitter
The rain is cold

As we walk home
Through the woods of old

There is a shadow
That follows us home

A memory of the past
Which is long forgotten

For what is legend
Is now myth

For what was forgotten
Has been relived

As time goes on
You are forgotten

This is how it was
This is how it is
And this is how it stays

You are forgotten
Only the lonely woods
Will know your name.

***Kayleigh Jones***

## She

She was born in 1952, with sisters yes,
Not one, but two.
She had a spirit wild and free
But then in 1963
When he wanted to be amused,
To her he came and sexually abused.
Her heart and soul were truly broken,
And from this nightmare, she's not woken.
Her life went on and all seemed well,
But there was no one she could tell
And as the years have passed her by,
She's lived her life in a total lie.
Her feelings and thoughts are so confused
By this man by whom she was sexually abused.
Can she go on living her life?
She's been a friend, a mother, a wife.
Maybe when she's 77 she'll find
True peace at the gates of Heaven.

***Maria Rousseau***

## Man On The Dole

Where has all the busyness and the
Industriousness of the steel works
And the coal mines of yesteryear gone?

Where is the man who drew his
Wage packet every week,
Feeling tired but with a good gut feeling inside,
Knowing he had done his job well?

The man? Oh he is still there,
But without the gut feeling,
Without the self-respect for being a working man.

Where is it all going to end?
All those downcast, glazed eyes,
All this soul-searching, dole-queuing.

You! You there!
*You tell me!*

***Shirley Gray***

## Politics

Damned by dreams that emasculate, whichever thoughts grow fond
A ritual that once grew great, before the broken bonds
Elevated past darkened doubt. Tattooed by streetlight fraud
The taxman knocks, reasons without. Civilian levy duly stored
Forgetting sinful syntax, forging sentences of stealth
Intricately evading tax and procuring piles of wealth.
To save their seats politicians lie, give bribes they don't resent
With starving hunger babies cry, while income tax is sorely spent
Witness wily officials in their Jaguars. Diamonds nested in wife's ears
Then see taxpayers in economy cars. They saved for years and years.
Will no one break the circle of lies and do the country a favour?
Recall the day democracy died. The birthday of New Labour.

***Kyle Hastings***

## TRAMP

Upon an old park bench I sit
Just a simple, broken man
I've roamed old England all my life
Only eating when I can

I have no friends to talk of
I have no home to rest
My life it has no meaning
Fulfilment, life or zest

But I'm proud of my old England
I fought in both its wars
But now death is awaiting
It's stretching out its claws

My body's week and feeble
The claws of death draw near
I wonder if they'll remember
They never will, I fear

Now I lay my head to rest
Never to wake
I wonder if my afterlife
Will be my lucky break.

***Martin Powers***

## A BROKEN HEART

*(This poem is dedicated to all the victims of a broken heart)*

A broken heart,
Such an odd expression
How to break something so vital
More like a wounded heart
My heart holds so many scars
Yours was just one more
So why does it feel like I'm dying inside again?
Maybe I am . . . unusual fate for me, Mr Cool and Cold
To die from a broken heart
Oh well . . . as the blackness comes to claim me
I wonder why is it I still love you
Even though the pain increases?
Simple, because I've got a broken heart . . .
Who'll fix me?

***Stephen James Thomas Lydall (17)***

## HARLECH CASTLE

Up on the hill and standing still
Fine in glow and strangely humourless
A cork on the hill cold in stone
As history comes in on the waves
Giving you back your land slowly, slowly

And holding the town together
With strong watching eyes
Embracing every traveller
With arms of hope

Yet the hill of the pilgrim is steep
One car at a time and single file on foot
As the sound of a harp chimes down on a scene
Where time stands still forever

And time travels slowly in history
From now till then
And the sweet music tells stories of heroes and foe
A place of such beauty on the Cambrian coast

Then the mist and rain sweep over the rooftops
Sailing down on our life
So bold in the morning
With sunshine smiling
And bragging about your breast
And years of watching and listening to the sea
Have made your mystery complete.

***Terrence Mark Allen***

## Tea Bowl By Ninsei (1647)

*(Discovered on a visit to Yoshi-ima, Gion, Kyoto, Japan, March 2000)*

Such a shiny, rough delight, as much for
eye as hand. The innards of this plain but
polished coarseness oozing light and
certainty, a sense of sureness, such that
it can captivate and mesmerise with its
sheeny coat of baked and glazed impurities.

And I thought I knew it all: the enamelled
jar by Ninsei, with the wisteria flower, my
favourite. The shock of this: I gaze, I lose
a heartbeat, forever I will see these things
a new-found, different way. Just another
bowl, I thought at first; it haunts the mind

and tears the sensitivities apart. A murky
mix from Ninsei's hands transmuted
into burnished bits of burnt browns
and ochres, spatters hardened in the
heat, this fragile, glistening glaze,
glowing in its modesty, floating in

its unpretentious stance. A luminosity
pervades this bowl. While Rembrandt
played with broody darks against the
shiny light, Ninsei's practised hands,
so many thousand miles away, fired
awesome shades as these.

Some bowl. Some bowl.
Discovery indeed.

***John Waterworth***

## A JOURNEY TO BEDFORD (VIA HAYNES)

In hot summer sun we
pass shorn fields, with
lines of washing
dancing in the breeze

Silent, sleepy cottages
in leafy lanes,
dappled shadows 'neath
trees in woodland glades

All the seats are filled,
people laughing and chatting
totally unaware of the
subtleties of nature

Fluffy clouds dot the sky
here and there. We rush on
past houses and barns,
cattle who stand and stare

Giant hangars stand proud
majestic and alone, whilst
opposite, builders, like ants,
are busy creating new homes

The last bit of countryside
is fading away, we rush
headlong into traffic, our
journey's over for today.

***L R Burton***

## Love

Like the petals of a red rose
Your love blossomed
And, by the time it grows.
Like the summer rain
That falls upon a flower,
Your love has grown,
Hour by hour.

The love you have
Has stood so strong.
Like the winds that sway,
You have shared it together,
Day by day.
It has never wilted,
It has never died,
Like a beautiful rose
That flourished and survived.

So Shirley and Brian
Here's our wish,
Happy 40th anniversary
Of
Wedded bliss.

***D Sherwood***

## I Remember One Day . . .

I remember one day, long ago,
Playing a game with my cousin
In the field across from my house.
Tossing an old plastic lid into the air
And hitting it with a stick,
With each throw
We would make a wish,
And if we hit the lid,
Our wishes would come true.
We played until nightfall.
My brother did marry that girl,
My sister did have another son,
But I'm older now
And I forget the rest.

***Eithne D Lonergan***

## THE FORGOTTEN ONE

As twilight falls, the forgotten one appears.
Loneliness and noiseless sounds he fears.
Shuffling along with a stoop, holding his bag by the loop,
He's alone.

He stops at shop windows, now dark,
And sees his reflection, so stark.
Videos and CDs hide in corners, with blank screens,
But he cares not for these,
Just friendship, and a voice that's serene.

But nobody cares, why should they?
He's dirty, he smells, and most do say,
'Children come here, don't go so near
To that old tramp, please keep away!'

The old man, he doesn't protest, after all, mother knows best.
He just carries on walking, alone and not talking,
Except to himself of course.

He once was a family man
And worked in the city, quite grand!
Now that's all gone, but the memory lives on.
He's not bitter, just needs someone's hand.

It can come to us all, and it's bad luck to fall
On hard times, in the bit city.
So please don't walk by, just stop and say 'Hi'
It costs nothing to show him some pity.

But alas it's not done, why should I be the one?
Why don't I just scurry on by?
But if you carry this thought, and your children be taught,
There but for the grace of God, go I.

***C Flack***

## A DAUGHTER

A tender, soft and female child
To make our lives complete
To bring in love and sunshine
To every day that we meet

The ribbons, frills and gurgles
Of a tiny baby girl
Will melt your heart
Like sun on snow
And leave your mind in a whirl

A daddy to protect her
This precious little thing
No one will ever harm her
My strength to her I'll bring

I'll ask each day for God above
To love and guide her light
The gentlest angels in the sky
To guard her soul at night

Welcome to this earth my child
I'll teach you all that I know
It will be my greatest pleasure
To slowly watch you grow

Like a flower in the sunshine
A rainbow in the haze
My tiny, newborn daughter
I will love you for always.

***Elizabeth Ann Crompton***

## A Silent World

As I finger-spell my name to a
Hearing child I pray
That perhaps she'll learn my sign language
To talk to me one day.

We laugh together, eat together,
Walk our dogs upon the downs,
But unless her face is facing me,
I cannot read her sounds!

I depend on clear lip pattern, good eyesight
And expressions on her face,
To gather information from this five-year-old
Called Grace.

My dear friend is her mother,
And we teach Grace very day,
That ears not working aren't a problem,
If we can understand what people say.

'I'll call you Auntie Hands,' said Grace,
'If you don't mind, 'cause you are my mate?'
'Well thank you, hearing friend,' I smiled
And signed thumbs up, 'That's great!'

***Nicola Goatcher***

## Entry In A Dream Diary

It was boring being asleep,
Without a single dream at stake,
So *boring - snoring* I lost all
Interest and eventually
I fell awake . . .

***Berto Smith***

## PEOPLE

Fireman,
Black and tan,
Publican,
Maths teacher,
Reverend preacher,
Shopkeeper,
Council worker,
Social shirker,
Zoo keeper,
Railway sleeper,
Airline pilot in the blue,
Taking passengers to Corfu.
Rhinestone cowboy
With lasso,
Solicitor trying to sue
Road sweeper,
Flower picker,
Poster sticker,
Video star,
Mechanic with motor car,
Tramp on the road,
Lorry driver with heavy load,
Driving instructor with
Highway Code.

***G Elson***

## LOOK AROUND

Look around at this wonderful world . . .
The trees, the sounds
They make their swirling
With the wind,
They send out energies
Of love
The birds, the bees and flowers
All have something
To give you
For what you see,
The beauty of them
*Is*
What *you* are
They come to be for
You, you
Alone
*You*
Asked for them,
They await your chord
Of knowing this
How beautiful they look
They too see your beauty
Realise you *are*
A part of them
Magical, forever changing
Becoming more.

***Kerrie Berroyer***

## My Garden

Come with me
And you will see
My flowers growing
By the tree.

There's daffs and tulips
And a rose,
Go up close
And with your nose

Smell the scent that lingers there,
Go on sniff
And smell the air.

Aren't the colours
Lovely too?
I wish that they
Just grew and grew.

There's the sunflower,
Oh what fun!
Pity that there's
Only one.
Still the size
Is truly rare,
10 metres tall,
Now that's not fair.

A child has come
And picked its head,
Well that one now
Is quite, quite dead.
All that work and all that toil,
Why can't they let them
Rest in soil?

***J F Hyde***

## Dear Kerry

Loving you was easy
It was the natural thing to do
When you were near me oh so close
It was my heart that flew
Were you really kissing me
Or was it just a dream
I want to have you near me
To quench my silent scream
I didn't want to say goodbye
Or even let you go
The words still throb within my head
When you told me *no!*
Why did you have to leave me?
Why did you go away?
I only wanted you with me
I wanted you to stay
I'm all alone now
With my broken heart
Looking at the view
Knowing the pain inside
Will never die
Until I have you.

***Jason Lewis***

## DREAMWORLD

When twilight falls and night descends,
and sleep evades me once again,
I drift into my world of fantasy,
enveloped amidst the countless characters
that I alone create.
Such webs they weave of love and hate,
truth and deception, despair and happiness.
Their ultimate destinies unknown, until I,
their creator,
delve into the turmoil of my mind.
Forever searching for some enlightenment,
whenever the evasiveness of sleep befalls me.

***Catherine Tidiman***

## Starlings

Smoke clouds
Swooping and vibrant, turn and roll
Feathery clouds pass like a scroll
Creating images at the dying day
Delighting in their fantasy display.

Rainbow colours
Shining and bright, breast purple patina
Lustrous plumage pure display,
As one they fly, without music they sing
Mimicked melodies, other birds bring.

Leafless trees
Cover their nakedness, pact
With moving shroud, mystery black
Starlings, their secrets undisclosed
Clandestine gathering, furtive host.

Like diamonds
A million stars gleam
In the evening sky
Beauty, flying free, flying high
Patterns of crystal clear shimmering.

Eerie shriek,
Dawn's early rise, they ascend as one
To a turquoise design, strong, mysterious
Fluttering throng, flit toward church spire
And city warm you satisfy a repast joy.

***Michael Maloney***

## War Song

A harrowing adventure for one too young,
Cheated of life yet showered in valour,
A drawn out end clung on and on,
Regroup boys and for God's sake sing a song.

There they lay upon muddied fields of terror,
Wondering why and for how long,
Trudging now with sunken heart,
Direction unknown, outcome improbable.

Tired bones and dreamy thoughts,
Of distant belles and memories,
Time becomes the enemy,
As tomorrow decides what it wants to be.

Etch a name unto a bullet,
Each man wondering who will get it,
Wrong time, wrong place,
Did you see the poor bugger's face?

It's the bravest act unknown to many,
Courage beyond the duty called for,
To stare him down every second of every day,
What a way to live and die,
I guess life didn't pass them by.

***A T Kay***

## Soul's Journey

Just a boy
A boy all his life
School
College
A house and wife.
Next is a sentence
Expected by all
To be fulfilled in the manner
Tradition calls for.
But the boy is crying
He cannot be told
His mind is alive
While his shell grows old.
He follows the path
That his conscience says to.
The world is aghast
So foolish
Eccentric.
Their eyes stay shut
All happy and clear
With no conscience to follow
There's no growing fear.
So they're safe
Oh so safe
Living life like it should
Until death
And then all again
Wherea's his may well end.

***Ben Thompson***

## End Of Our Love

Numbing pain
Ripping violently
Through my heart
Yet again

You think it's dead
But love explodes
Through your totally
F****d-up head

Physical agony
I can't describe
When will this pain
Ever subside?

Want it back
All that we had,
Cos I can't go on living
Feeling this bad

We had it all
Dreams can come true
But you left
And my dreams left with you

Who believes love conquers all?
You sad, naïve, pitiful fool.

***N R Finnis***

## POWERFUL TRUTH

This today is the first day
Of the rest of my new life . . .
Eyes wide open, heart confident
Of love and health full of wisdom
That gives wealth within
The prize is unreachable
And no money can buy within.

Love and health are the
Heartbeats of life
Without these we crumble into a heap
And fall into a life-long sleep . . .
Awake is like a bad dream
We can't run from
Can't wake from,
Can't belong in any way . . .
We fail to be.

We edge past the danger
And still asleep
Blinded by the drop beneath
Taken we fall deep . . .
The darkness of our minds
We find nothing but sleep
Restless and depressed
By nothingness cut deep
Blood seeps . . .
The energy we can't seem to keep.

But today I woke from an eternal sleep
And made dreams part of reality
Even if they don't extend as part of me
I will have seen a sign to be me . . .
Me and all I see.

Alive to strive forever
Never holding back
Or rough by the hurt we felt
While I was asleep . . .
Blessed be . . . me.

Purple lily

***Julia Brereton***

## Paper Mache

Scuffle love blew in the wind forlorn,
Passion stirred foreign.
Hung out like strips of white satin, in tatters.
Jelly legs on the burst mattress.
Pharmaceutical beauty, why worry,
Nothing's fashion.
I've made a life out of paper mache.
Baby shambles, we could steal
Glances and feel embarrassed.
As the wind flies against us
We'll walk through streets of plastic,
Our hearts bursting full of purpose.
We belong and tingle in grey matter.
Throwing stones at the mirror water,
Burying fossils, laying all night on benches
Under the stars of paper mache.

***Colin Beck***

## Ode To Beauty

a flattered glance, a whispered thought
a glimpse perchance, a wondered aught
a feeling, a presence, a passing essence
a quintessence,
a fluttering iridescence of coloured flight,
soundless, silent, nothing evident of passing things,
a fleeting thither of wings,
of colour and light, as though impossible of flight,
but godlike beauty and majestic might,
are mirrored in this carefree sight,
as the sun shines through a meadow's haze,
all stop to wonder at nature's coloured maze,
as it goes by, the mind digresses,
and frees itself of stresses that exist within,
goes on high, thanking God as it gazes on
the miracle of a butterfly.

***K Dennett***

## YOUR PICTURE BOOK

Life is like a picture book
Made by you for you
To step inside and browse around
When you have nothing else to do
When you are old and getting lonely
Maybe a bit downcast
Open up your book inside your head
And see what's in the past
It started really the day you were born
Unbeknown to you
Keeping a record from day one
Of everything you do
First it's pictures that you see
Before the stories all unfold
Some of them have been there for so long
And never been retold
So many stories
So many scenes
Too many to recount
But all are in your picture book
Of this I have no doubt
Now if the pictures that you see
All seem sad and lonely
Just keep on searching and you'll find
One, meant for your eyes only.

***D J Fryer***

## MEN, MEN, MEN

To clear my life of men right now
would really clear my head
I don't know who will turn up next
I'm confused with what I have said

To start afresh right here, right now
would make me feel so great
if a loving handsome man turned up
I could not resist a date.

Too many men at one time now
what mayhem this has turned out to be
it started feeling very good
now I don't think it funny

Men at work, men at home
men everywhere I go
I must have some kind of loving spell
because they won't leave me alone

Shall I have a break from them
and turn into a nun?
I do not think so darling
because I am really having fun.

Picture me in ten years time
a worn-out, haggard chick!
With men still drooling after me
I wonder what's my trick?

***Christine Noah***

## 'Tis Love

What is love? This beguiler of the heart,
That plays sweet music like cherub's harp.
And with fancy cast; leads the senses to dreams afar,
And if found wanting, bleeds the flesh with a cut so sharp.

What dost thou wish, love of many: born of a woman? Conceived by man?
The gift of a god! Or the piercing aim of a cherub's plan.
Why dost thou lead my heart astray; betwixt two fluttering doves,
I am weak and easily hurt - I wish I was so easily loved.

But take heed the love of selfish gain, and the bitter taste from whence it came,
Sweet at first, but sickly after; a compassion of oneself will mourn thereafter.
For love should be shared not selfish gained, and yet if love be shared,
Would it not be selfish? For all we regret is what we did not love,
And what we mourn cannot touch. Only flesh regrets.

But alas, if love be found, find within it truth. Cherish it to thine soul:
And to be sure, with every kiss, as the heart leaps abound to know such bliss.
Hold it as a child, gentle to the lips; kiss its brow as a child would wish.
With love, take faith, the hearts so dear, love whispers sweet echoes with melodies near.
Let not love's tears cry through dreams. Like a star, behold; confine its love,
It gave birth to light to shine from above. Do not leave it to be alone, cherish -

'Tis love.

***Nomad***

## The Alcoholic

I have reached the depths, the lowest depths,
Yet cannot find that which I seek to find.
What brought me to this state of mind?
What state of mind, have I a mind? I have a body
That's carried by tired and unwilling legs,
To find and drink the dregs.
The dregs that make these almost sightless eyes
Search and gaze for the end of this maze.
My world is just an endless maze.
How did I find this maze? Why do I strive to lose
Myself in its ever-winding path, each turning wrong.
I don't belong.
Feverishly I tread this path in hope to find
That which I seek. My senses shout . . .
God, let me out.
What brought me to this state of no return,
This endless void? The reason's gone,
I just go on.
And only know the night is cold, the day too long,
I struggle on,
I pray with every breath,
For death.

***John Tovey***

## Our Ruby Wedding

As we walk down life's path
Sometimes we cry, sometimes we laugh,
And as we look through the tears
We can see the happy years
So take away the sorrow and the pain
We will return again
Happiness you will find
Is a memory left behind.
Our mind is a camera view
Of things we used to do.
Not knowing when we met
The pattern of our destiny is set,
The children born and then they are gone
To find their own paths to travel on.
Now our steps are very slow.
We hope there are more paths to go.

***Marlene Barnett***

## Dark November Night

Dark November night,
Saturday slanting rain;
Cold news about a friend.

Veiled vision perceived,
Blindness transpires:
Desperation of moods.

Helplessness ensues,
Confusion reigns,
Weeping commences.

Confined in a faraway place,
Unable to see.
But what of the friend's friend?

***David Lees***

## THE LAND OF NO NAMES

Out there, in the darkness, lie the souls of good men,
Their duty paid,
Their screams return to you again, once more, and again,
The rats begin their bloody raid,
On the bodies that lie in the land of no names.

The air around spreads disease and horror beneath,
The stars guide those
Who are now honoured with a wreath,
Your mind you must not close,
And forget those that lie in the land of no names.

Bullets, shells and mines can kill,
But the bodies on the barbed wire
Give the blood a chill,
The souls rise higher
Away from the bodies in the land of no names.

A bugle and a whistle give a foreboding sign,
As the troops prepare,
The weather is fine,
But we buried them there,
The men with no name, in the land of no names.

***Ben Falshaw (15)***

## The Last Days

My life of late is full of dreams,
but dreams are fine, or so it seems.

Limbs that work with startling ease,
whilst I lay still and gently wheeze.

And life is young and beautiful still,
that first romance to tease and thrill.

Time means nothing, what's it matter?
Just memories fond of laughs and chatter.

A hand in mine, that field, that lane,
see the sunrise, feel the rain.

And yet each day I'm sinking fast,
each dream I dream could be my last.

Another night, another dawn,
another pill, another yawn.

Then mornings filled with mist and clutter,
a voice sometimes, 'You stupid nutter?'

But care I not to have a friend,
for dreams are mine, and mine to the end.

***P Jennison***

# THE THINGS I TOOK FOR GRANTED

The things I took for granted -
Long ago when I was young:
The bluebelled, primrosed woodlands
And fields in which to run.

The tadpoled ponds to skitter on;
The stepping stones, those summer songs;
The laughing brooks, those first love looks -
Have sadly all but gone.

Oh! Take me back sweet zephyr wings,
Take me back I pray;
For the things I took for granted -
Have sadly gone away.

Was life so full of innocence
Seen through the eyes of youth?
Or was it just enlightenment -
Having had first sight of truth?

Still my heart and soul will always stay,
And my spirit fore'er in fields will play:
In woodlands that the golden primrose gild,
And glades that royal bluebells filled -
Are with me to this day;
For the things I took for granted -
Have sadly gone away.

***Roger Oldfield***

## WE PROMISED THAT

We promised that we'll leave this land
to travel far across the sand
to forget the past and be one hand
to never have somewhere to land

the days have passed and so the years

we promised that we'll beat the tears
to stay aware and kill the beast
to be so strong and have no fears

the days have passed and so the years

the tears seem to win, and we are so weak
the beast grew up, and so the fears
the same land, across the years.

***Hosam Haitham Al Dahhan***

## DÉJÀ-VU

Time passes,
Mind tells lies,
But memories never die.
People, friendships, grow - mature and wither away
Like a bluebell in the rain - it's there, then fades away.
But ghosts linger on for all time,
Reliving an era that's way gone by.

'Déjà-vu - what's that you say?
I've been here on a previous day?'
'How long ago was that you think?'
'Oh! I know the time, date and place,
It tries to blur and fade away,
But it comes back hooting and puffing on another day.'
'Do you feel sad and oh so blue?'
'All of that and joy - yes joy too.'
'Why be joyful at the passing of a friend?'
'It's sad, joyful and a blessing too,
For I can reinvent you.'

'So déjà-vu come ye forth
In a sunny day a long lost cloud has come home to stay
The sky is again the same
And the days of the week and the dates are now as then.'

'Yes I was here that day,
Your friend - you and I
I've come home to stay
To take you back to those joyful days
And take away this sadness and your tears.'

A shady place - a gentle breeze
Gently blowing green leaves
Take me to that joyful time
Away from this harsh, cruel, menacing time.
Time passes,
Mind tells lies,
But memories never die.

***Raymond P G Rapson***

## MIRAGE

A teardrop hangs
suspended in hours,
A minute frozen
falls within showers,
A smile caught
amid golden spray,
A sparkle captured
in sun's ice-cold ray,
Two lovers laugh
herald the morn,
A perfect world
yet one so worn,
One with no place
for laughter or tears,
One where reality
is all of our fears.

***Kyra Reynolds***

## WHITE

White is peaceful, pale and passionate.
I see angels spreading their wings through the silky, pearly sky.

White is splashy,
It's milk pouring into a glass,
You can feel the gentle breeze blowing against your cheeks.

I see opal rings glistening,
White is the silence of snowflakes on the window listening.

White is the designer's modern minimal,
White is the lily dewdrops of morning,
White is the spirit your name is calling.

***Natalie Amy Anne Jones (11)***

## FRIENDSHIP

Silence, it takes awhile to get going.
How can you expect to get on one that rockets by
Chasing an aura that leaves you in a spin
And the typhoon washes away expectations.

I'll get the next one and meet up down the line.
Confused and all alone, the warmth banished,
No shelter, there's a strike of lightning,
The thunder screeches to a halt, you're going nowhere.

Sometimes you're lucky, the windows reflect the sun.
Take another look, you might want to know what's inside.
Protective it may be to sit in first class,
While the Cheshire cat reassures the feeling you're safe.

What a lazy feeling, to get off from time to time.
Relax; it's no fairground ride.
Life dictates and we're torn apart,
But the shimmering light dims the end of the line.

Locked on the rails that run forever.
Accompanied by others that shine; fortunately.
Some may leave and never return,
While the ones that stay are your noble playmates.

***Stephen Alan Smith***

## Deity

When rugged rocks encircle space and time
And eagles soar on spirit wings
To embrace the simple gifts of life
The sweetness of a blade of grass
The mist beyond a waterfall
Then I see infinity
Is just as real as life and breath
And death is just rebirth, that's all.

Now orbs of light reach out to dance
As prisms on the Scottish shores
The Highland mysteries bear fruit
Of angels' tears and ancient scores
Awoken from predestined sleep
Yet shrouded in simplicity
Then, light shall guide the lost souls home
And truth will set the prisoner free.

***Deanna L Mills***

## A New Millennium

As we head to a new millennium,
There should be a guiding light,
To teach our new generation
Not the wrong, but the right.
To share and be humble,
To be happy and not mumble.
Let there be peace on our land,
Stand side by side and hold each and one another's hand.
The last 100 years have seen many tears,
Titanic, two world wars, Gulf and Argentinean wars,
There's been fighting in all corners of the globe,
There's also been happiness and cheers,
With new inventions, science and cures,
New medicines to help our poor and sick.
If everybody in this country and afar
Could live together in peace and harmony,
We could teach our next generation
What it is like to live happily.
No fighting, greed, vandalism, crime or violence,
But to be helpful to one another,
To have the time to help those in need,
And not to expect to be paid for our good deed.
Let the aged go out when they like,
Without the fear of being mugged,
Let the lasses go out at night for their fun,
Without the risk of meeting a man with a gun.
If everyone, black or white, Asian or other,
Young or old, it does not matter,
Could live together in peace and not war,
The next millennium will be worth living for.

***David Skinner***